ASTRONOMY

by
TERRY MAHONEY

WHAT IS ASTRONOMY?

How big is the universe? What is it made of? How old is it? Is there life on other planets? People have always been interested in the night sky. We wonder exactly what makes up the huge area of space. *Astronomy* (as • **trô** • nə • mē) is the science that observes the universe and tries to answer these questions. Many different areas of scientific study are part of astronomy. *Planetary* (**pla** • nə • tā • rē) *science* is the study of planets. *Cosmology* (käz • **mä** • lə • jē) is the study of how the universe was formed. *Exobiology* (ek • sō • bī • ä • lə • jē) is the study of life in the universe. *Astrophysics* (as • trō • **fi** • ziks) is the study of how things work in space.

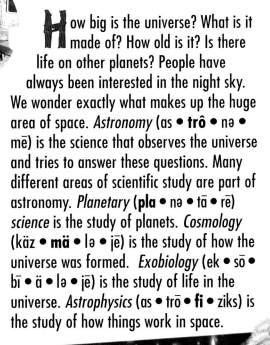

THE STUDY OF THE PLANETS

Planetary science is the branch of astronomy that studies the planets. Planetary scientists also research other smaller objects in our solar system. It brings together parts of *chemistry* (**ke** • mə • strē), *physics* (**fi** • ziks), *geology* (jē • **ä** • lə • jē), and *meteorology* (mē • tē • ər • **ä** • lə • jē). For the last 40 years, manned and unmanned spaceships have been sent into space. Astronauts have walked on the moon. Missions like Spacelab (*above*) have been launched high into Earth's orbit to observe objects in space. Unmanned space *satellites* (**sa** • tə • līts) and other machines continue to change planetary science. They have visited distant worlds in our solar system. The satellites send back information to eager astronomers on Earth.

POSITIONAL ASTRONOMY

The very first thing we need to know about an astronomical object is where to find it. We also need to know how it moves in space. Before the invention of the *telescope* (**te** • lə • skōp), astronomers used tools such as this *armillary* (**är** • mə • lā • rē) *sphere* (sfēr) to find their way around the night sky. Now, astronomers use telescopes and satellites to find the exact positions of stars and planets in the sky. They also use these tools to track objects' movements.

THE BIG QUESTIONS

Cosmology is the branch of astronomy that looks at the universe as a whole. It became a science during the first half of the 20th century. The general theory of *relativity* (re • lə • **ti** • və • tē) was created by Albert Einstein (1879–1955). It helped cosmology develop. His theory explains how galaxies, black holes, and even the universe change the space surrounding them (as shown in the center of the above picture). Today, cosmologists ask questions about exactly how the universe came into being. They also want to know how it might come to an end.

ARE WE ALONE?

Many of us believe that there probably is other life in the universe. Since the 1950s, radio, television, and magazines (such as this one) have added to these ideas by describing imagined alien life forms. Exobiology (or *astrobiology* [as • trō • bī • ä • lə • jē]) is the branch of astronomy that looks at the chances of finding life on other planets. There is still a possibility that life will be found on Mars. Another possible place there may be life is Europa, a moon of Jupiter. Europa might have oceans able to support life under its icy crust.

STARGAZING

Astrophysics began in the 1860s, after several chemical elements were identified in the sun and other stars. The name means simply "the physics of the stars." This type of astronomy looks at starlight. This can help explain the structure and growth of galaxies. Astrophysicists have made many important discoveries. For example, they studied the long, dark dust lanes of the brilliant Whirlpool galaxy (*above*). They found out that the dust lanes are actually nurseries for future generations of stars.

TRICKS & METHODS

In 1609, the Italian astronomer Galileo moved astronomy forward when he used a homemade telescope to view the sky. Today, astronomers can launch probes deep into the solar system to send back new facts. Space telescopes also send back huge amounts of information on the stars and galaxies. Telescopes are all built to do two things: collect as much light as possible and provide the most detailed images (pictures). Both of these things depend on the size of the collecting lens or mirror.

SPACE PROBES

Unfortunately it will not be possible for humans to visit many parts of the solar system because it is very dangerous. However, robots can go where humans can't. Astronomers have sent robotic probes—machines that gather information—to planets in the solar system and beyond. These probes send images to Earth using radio signals from TV cameras. Other onboard instruments take a range of measurements.

RADIO TELESCOPES

Radio telescopes were first used in the 1940s to search for radio signals coming from space. Many objects in the universe, from stars to galaxies, *emit* (give off) radio waves. Radio telescopes are be bigger than ordinary telescopes. This is because radio waves are longer than light waves. Radio telescopes must be larger to capture the same amount of detail. Radio waves can pass through dust clouds that block visible light. They have been used to map the Milky Way (see pages 22–23).

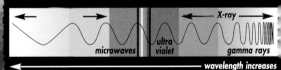

microwaves | ultra violet | X-ray | gamma rays

wavelength increases

SCIENCE EXPLAINED: THE ELECTROMAGNETIC SPECTRUM

Light is a form of radiation that is carried in waves. Each of the colors of the rainbow has its own wavelength. The entire range of wavelengths is called the electromagnetic (i • lek • trō • mag • ne • tik) spectrum. Earth's atmosphere cuts out many of the wavelengths, protecting us. From space, the entire spectrum can be collected by telescopes. Astronomers can learn a lot about objects by studying what kind of radiation they send out. For example, they can study the object's density (bulk or mass), temperature, chemical composition, and movement.

HUBBLE SPACE TELESCOPE

Space telescopes have changed how astronomy is done. The atmosphere of the Earth is a problem for astronomers. It makes the picture we see through a telescope tremble and ripple like the surface of a pond. It is this that makes the stars twinkle. In space, however, there is no atmosphere. Launched in 1990, the Hubble Space Telescope orbits about 370 miles (600 km) above the Earth. It sends back very clear pictures to astronomers.

REFLECTING TELESCOPES

Today, most telescopes built for research use mirrors instead of lenses to collect light. Mirrors have several advantages over lenses. Lenses create false colors, absorb light, and can sag under their own weight. However, mirrors do not have such problems.

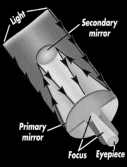

Light

Secondary mirror

Primary mirror

Focus   Eyepiece

1. Light falls through the top of the open-frame tube, and heads toward the primary mirror.

2. The light is then reflected up the tube to the smaller, secondary mirror.

3. The light is then reflected back down the tube. It passes through a hole in the primary mirror to the focus (located beneath the primary mirror).

REFRACTING TELESCOPES

Objective lens

Focus

Eyepiece

1. The objective lens catches the light and brings it into focus.

2. The eyepiece magnifies the focused image.

Refracting telescopes have two lenses. The one at the front is called the objective lens. The other, at the back, is called the eyepiece. The eyepiece magnifies the focused and improved image. Today, these are less popular with professional astronomers than reflecting telescopes. *Binoculars* (bə • nä • kyə • lürz) are small twin refracting telescopes arranged side by side. They are popular with amateur astronomers.

WINTER SKY

Orion, the Hunter (marked below in red), is an amazing *constellation* (kän • stə • lā • shən), a particular group of stars. Orion is visible during late evenings in winter. The three stars in Orion's belt can be used as a signpost in the sky. Just below the belt is a shiny patch called the Orion *Nebula* (**ne** • byə • lə). It is a wonderful sight through binoculars or a small telescope. The Orion Nebula is, in fact, a nursery where stars are being born right now.

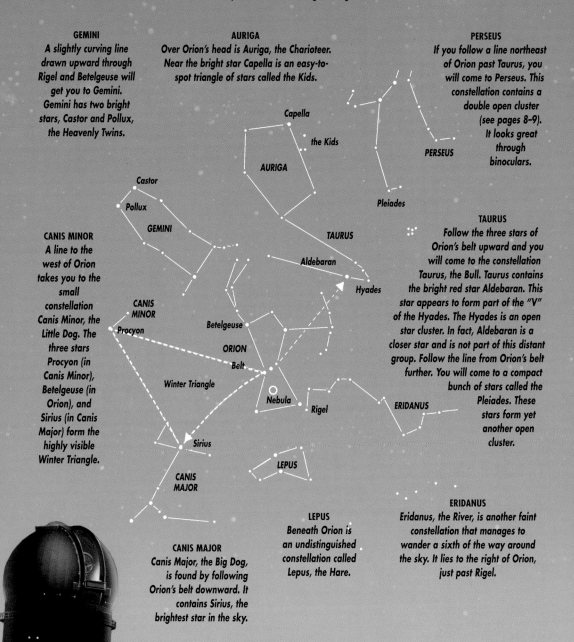

GEMINI
A slightly curving line drawn upward through Rigel and Betelgeuse will get you to Gemini. Gemini has two bright stars, Castor and Pollux, the Heavenly Twins.

AURIGA
Over Orion's head is Auriga, the Charioteer. Near the bright star Capella is an easy-to-spot triangle of stars called the Kids.

PERSEUS
If you follow a line northeast of Orion past Taurus, you will come to Perseus. This constellation contains a double open cluster (see pages 8–9). It looks great through binoculars.

CANIS MINOR
A line to the west of Orion takes you to the small constellation Canis Minor, the Little Dog. The three stars Procyon (in Canis Minor), Betelgeuse (in Orion), and Sirius (in Canis Major) form the highly visible Winter Triangle.

TAURUS
Follow the three stars of Orion's belt upward and you will come to the constellation Taurus, the Bull. Taurus contains the bright red star Aldebaran. This star appears to form part of the "V" of the Hyades. The Hyades is an open star cluster. In fact, Aldebaran is a closer star and is not part of this distant group. Follow the line from Orion's belt further. You will come to a compact bunch of stars called the Pleiades. These stars form yet another open cluster.

CANIS MAJOR
Canis Major, the Big Dog, is found by following Orion's belt downward. It contains Sirius, the brightest star in the sky.

LEPUS
Beneath Orion is an undistinguished constellation called Lepus, the Hare.

ERIDANUS
Eridanus, the River, is another faint constellation that manages to wander a sixth of the way around the sky. It lies to the right of Orion, just past Rigel.

NAVIGATING THE NIGHT SKY

On a clear, moonless night, over 2,000 stars can be seen with the naked eye. Ancient astronomers identified star patterns, called constellations. These patterns are purely a human invention. They help people find their way in the sky. In reality, what looks to us like a bright star might really be a dim nearby star. A truly bright star might appear dim to us because of its huge distance from Earth.

CEPHEUS
A straight line through Merak and Dubhe in the Big Dipper and Polaris will take you to Cepheus, a dim constellation.

SPRING SKY

When you look up at the late evening sky in spring, you should be able to see seven bright stars in the Big Dipper. Use them (marked below in red) to navigate your way around the sky.

CASSIOPEIA
A line from Mizar in the Big Dipper through Polaris takes you to the constellation Cassiopeia. Parts of the Milky Way pass through this "W"-shaped constellation.

DRACO
Between Ursa Major and Ursa Minor is long, winding Draco, the Dragon. Draco is a fairly dim constellation.

URSA MINOR
Follow the two stars Merak and Dubhe in the Big Dipper north and you will come to Polaris, the Pole Star. It is in the constellation Ursa Minor, the Little Bear. Ursa Minor is also called the Little Dipper.

BOOTES
The three left-hand stars of the Big Dipper can be used to trace a gentle curve downward. Follow this curve to the bright orange star Arcturus in the constellation Bootes, the Herdsman.

URSA MAJOR & THE BIG DIPPER
The Big Dipper, or Seven Stars, is not actually a constellation. It represents the brightest part of the constellation Ursa Major, the Big Bear. The most important thing about this constellation is that some of its stars make useful signposts to other parts of the sky.

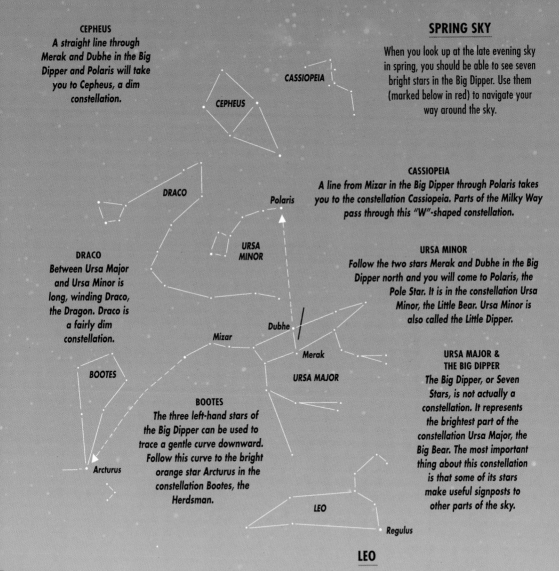

LEO

Directly underneath the Big Dipper is the constellation Leo, the Lion. It is one of the few constellations that looks even a little like its name. Its bright star, Regulus, is the dot in a reversed question mark of stars known as the Sickle.

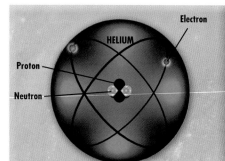

HELIUM

Electron

Proton

Neutron

ATOMS & MOLECULES

All known matter is made of atoms. Atoms are a bit like tiny solar systems. They have a central *nucleus* (**nū • klē • əs**) and *electrons* that go around the nucleus like planets orbiting the sun. The nucleus is usually made of two kinds of particles (bits that make up matter): *protons* and *neutrons* (**nū • trônz**). Normally, there are as many orbiting electrons as there are protons in the nucleus. Sometimes an atom loses one or more of its electrons. It is then said to be *ionized*. The two most important atoms in astronomy are *helium* (*see above*) and *hydrogen* (*see below*). Helium has two orbiting electrons and a nucleus of two protons and two neutrons. Hydrogen has a single proton in its nucleus and a single orbiting electron. In space, hydrogen atoms are either found as individual atoms or as atoms stuck together as *molecules* (**mä • lə • kyūlz**). Helium remains a free-floating atom. A gas of ionized atoms is called *plasma*. Most of the visible matter in the universe is in plasma form. Plasmas are said to be the fourth state of matter (the other three forms are solid, liquid, and gas).

HYDROGEN

Electron

Proton

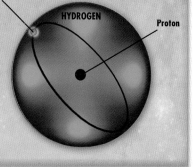

BUILDING BLOCKS OF THE UNIVERSE

Astronomy asks many big questions, such as: What is the universe made of? How did it all begin? and Why do stars shine? However, to understand these big ideas, it is necessary to simplify things. Astronomers can begin to piece together the universe by studying the smallest units that make up matter—atoms and elements. Everything is made up of the same simple elements. Many of the things that happen at the tiny atomic level can lead to major events in the universe. For example, the atomic events that cause a hydrogen bomb to explode also cause the stars to shine.

FROM SMALL BEGINNINGS

Atoms are the smallest independent units that make up the chemistry of the universe. Some combine in clumps called molecules. Both atoms and molecules float freely in the space between the stars. There are also dust grains, which come off of giant stars. These tiny dust grains each measure a thousandth of a millimeter across. They combine to form truly enormous clouds such as the Horsehead Nebula (*above*). These clouds are actually star factories. Eventually, the gas and dust in them fall inward to create new stars.

SCIENCE EXPLAINED: LIGHT YEARS

Distances in astronomy are way too big to use measurements like miles or kilometers. Astronomers use a unit of measurement called a light year instead. Light travels 186,000 miles (300,000 km) per second. In other words, it could whip around the Earth seven times in a single second. A light year is 6 million, million miles, which is how far light travels in a year.

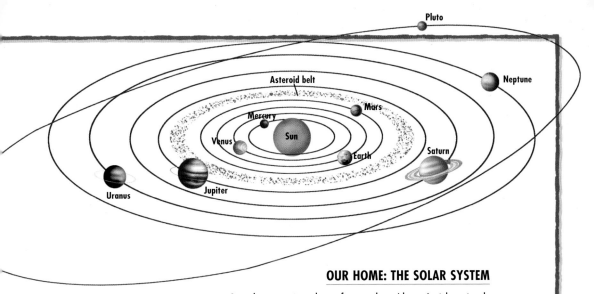

OUR HOME: THE SOLAR SYSTEM

Our solar system is made up of a central star (the sun), eight major planets, minor planets, *asteroids* (**as** • tə • rō̄ē dz), and *comets* (icy rocks). Comets throw out tails of gas and dust when they fall toward the sun. All the stars you see in the night sky lie beyond our solar system. Our galaxy is called the *Milky Way*. There are countless other galaxies.

STAR GROUPINGS

Stars contain most of the visible matter in the universe. Stars are giant balls of hot gas. They are grouped together in a number of different ways, described below.

OPEN CLUSTERS
Stars spend their first years in stellar nurseries, called open clusters, with up to 10,000 other stars. Open clusters are gradually pulled apart by the gravity of their surroundings. Then all the stars float freely in space. The nearest star to the sun is just over four light years away.

GLOBULAR CLUSTERS
Globular (**glô** • byə • lər) clusters can contain up to a million old stars. They can be ten times the size of open clusters. The stars in globular clusters are tightly held by gravity. About 140 globular clusters (like the NGC 1850 shown at right) surround our galaxy.

GALAXIES
Galaxies (above) are the biggest single units in the universe. Our own galaxy measures 100,000 light years across and contains more than 100 billion stars.

GALAXY CLUSTERS
Galaxies do not float freely in space but form clusters of galaxies. The Milky Way is part of a group of 31 known galaxies called the Local Group. This galaxy measures about 6 million light years across. Clusters of galaxies (left) can form larger clusters called superclusters.

THE BIRTH OF A STAR

All stars are born from clouds of dust, and end their lives in spectacular fashion. They begin life as dwarfs. As they heat up, they change into giants or supergiants. Depending on how much *mass* (weight) they start out with, they end their lives in a variety of different ways.

1. New stars all come from giant clouds of dust and gas.

2. Knots begin to form in the gas cloud as gravity pulls it together. This squeezing causes the cloud to heat up.

3. Eventually the gas begins to spin around. Jets of gas shoot out of the poles.

4. The star's brightness increases as a nuclear reaction begins at its center. All the gas and dust in the space surrounding the star is blown away. Finally the star emerges from its dusty cocoon.

5. The process is complete. The new dwarf star begins to shine, and joins the main group of stars. This is the most stable period of a star's life.

THE DEATH OF A STAR

W hether a dwarf has changed into a giant or a supergiant determines how the star will die...

THE STELLAR FAMILY

Astronomers plot stars on a chart called the Hertzsprung-Russell diagram. A star's place on the chart depends on its brightness and temperature. Once a dwarf star has formed and begun turning its hydrogen into helium, it joins the *main sequence*. The main sequence is a strip on this graph that most stars in the universe (including our sun) lie on. Giants and supergiants are bright stars that lie above the main sequence. Although they have fairly cool surface temperatures, they are bright because they have a huge surface area. Betelgeuse in Orion (see pages 6–7) is an example of a supergiant. It has a diameter hundreds of times that of our sun! White dwarfs are stars located in the bottom left of the graph. They are incredibly hot, but quite dim.

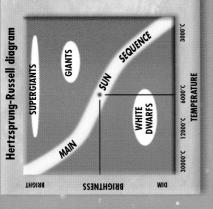

Hertzsprung-Russell diagram

SUPERGIANTS

GIANTS

SUN

MAIN
SEQUENCE

WHITE
DWARFS

BRIGHT — DIM
BRIGHTNESS

30000°C   12000°C   6000°C   3000°C
TEMPERATURE

SUPERGIANTS

A supergiant starts its life as a main sequence dwarf, but it is much brighter, hotter, and heavier than the Sun. Also, it can be hundreds of times bigger. It has a chaotic but very short life.

1. Like a dwarf, a supergiant starts its life on the main sequence, but it is much hotter and brighter. It can be hundreds of times the diameter of the Sun.

2. After a brilliant but short career, a supergiant dies in a spectacular explosion called a supernova. This explosion is so bright that it can outshine all the other stars in the galaxy together.

3. A supernova leaves behind a very dense object such as a neutron star or a black hole (see pages 24–25).

GIANTS

A giant is a former dwarf that has cooled and expanded to a great size. In 5,000 million years from now, this will happen to our sun. As a result, Mercury and Venus will become part of the growing sun. When that happens, Earth's atmosphere and oceans will boil away.

1. If a star uses all the hydrogen in its central core, hydrogen burning will start to happen in the inner layers. These layers will become heated and cause the outer layer of the star to swell outwards.

2. As a giant's inside gets hotter and hotter, it eventually puffs away its swollen outer shell. This is called a planetary nebula.

3. The hot object left behind after a giant has passed the planetary nebula stage is called a white dwarf. The gravity of white dwarfs is so intense that the result is a very dense Earth-sized object. The white dwarf is so dense that a handful of its material would weigh several tons.

Solar wind

Magnetic field

A GIANT MAGNET

The Earth is unusual. It has a fairly strong magnetic field, which acts like a bar magnet at its center. This magnetic field serves as a shield against charged particles from the sun (called the *solar wind*). Such particles are deadly to life, so we owe our continued existence to the Earth's magnetic field. However, when there are particularly violent storms on the sun, the charged particles become a danger to astronauts. They can even pass through the upper atmosphere. When this happens, the solar wind causes radio interference, power outages, and the northern lights.

HIDE & SEEK

The moon orbits the Earth at an average distance of 240,000 miles (384,400 km). For half of its orbit it is closer to the sun than the Earth. For the other half it is farther away. This means that it shows different portions of its lit surface to the Earth at different times. This gives us what are known as the *lunar* (**lū** • nər) phases. However, the moon completes one spin on its axis in the same time that it takes to orbit the Earth. This means it always shows the same face to the Earth. This picture was taken by the Apollo 17 astronauts. It shows the borderline separating day and night on the moon.

THE WORLD OF THE MOON

The moon's surface is divided into bright highlands and dark volcanic lava plains. The entire surface has many craters caused by *meteorite* (**mē** • tē • ə • rīt) hits. The moon is an airless world. There is no liquid water on its surface. This means that the surface is exactly as it was millions of years ago. The Apollo astronauts left *seismometers* (sīz • **mä** • mi • tərz) to measure tremors on the lunar surface. These have recorded "moonquakes" 500 miles (800 km) underground.

EARTH & MOON: A DOUBLE ACT

Many of the planets in the solar system have moons. Our own planet is no exception. What is special about our moon is its size compared to Earth's size. All the other moons in the solar system are much smaller than their central planets. The Earth has a special relationship with its moon. This relationship affects aspects of life on our planet. The moon's *gravitational* (gra • və • **tā** • shən • əl) *pull* (the invisible force keeping the two bodies together) is mainly responsible for tides. It is also slowly affecting the length of our days.

THE THIRD PLANET

The Earth is the third planet from the sun. It orbits the sun once a year at a mean distance of 93 million miles (150 million km). It is over five times denser than water. The Earth's pole-to-pole diameter is less than its diameter measured at the equator. This slight squashing at the poles is due to the daily rotation. It causes the Earth to bulge outward at the equator. This breathtaking view was taken by the crew of the Apollo 17 space mission.

A HAVEN FOR LIFE

Look at the picture above. What can you see? Clouds? Oceans? Plants? What you see creates the things needed for life—water and carbon dioxide. These features have given Earth special conditions that have allowed life to thrive. Astronomers look for water and carbon-based elements in the hope of finding planets that could support life. The Earth is also important for astronomers hoping to understand the make-up of similar planets in our solar system. Geologists know the deep structure of the inside of the Earth from measuring *seismic* (**sīz** • mik) waves from earthquakes. Astronomers can use this information to develop a better understanding of the other Earthlike planets.

SCIENCE EXPLAINED: TIDES & GRAVITY

The level of Earth's oceans rises and falls twice a day. These changes are called the tides. Tides are caused by the combined gravitational pull of the moon and sun. The moon's pull is a lot stronger, so the oceans swell into the shape of a football. There is a buildup of water on the side facing the moon. There is another water buildup on the opposite side of the Earth. As the Earth rotates on its axis, different parts of the oceans are raised. The water does not move forward or back, as you might think, but actually rises and falls twice a day. Tides are not the only way in which the moon affects our planet. The pull of its gravity is slowing down the Earth's rotation. This gradually makes our days longer. It is also slowly pushing the moon farther away from the Earth.

EARTHLIKE PLANETS

The four closest planets to the sun—Mercury, Venus, Earth, and Mars—form a family of small, dense rocky worlds known as the *terrestrial* (tə • **tres** • trē • əl) planets. They are called "terrestrial" because of their similarity to Earth. People have studied these planets with telescopes for centuries. However, it was not until the 1950s that astronomers were able to piece together the complicated past history of our solar system. Each planet has turned out to be *unique* (different and individual) and has provided astronomers with many surprises.

GREAT BALL OF FIRE

Venus is a forbidding and harsh world. It orbits the sun once every 224.7 Earth days at a distance of 67 million miles (108 million km). Until Russian and American space probes reached it, little was known about this fiery world. This was because Venus's entire surface is permanently covered by thick clouds. A dense atmosphere of carbon dioxide traps the heat from the sun. This produces temperatures high enough to melt lead. Orbital radar probes were used by astronomers to make a complete map of the surface of Venus. It has craters, volcanoes, and mountains.

MR. SPOCK & THE PLANET VULCAN

The orbit of Mercury does not quite obey Newton's theory of gravity. In 1860, the French astronomer Urbain de Leverrier studied this problem. His results suggested that an undiscovered planet was inside the orbit of Mercury. This planet was pulling Mercury off course. He named the supposed new planet Vulcan. Another astronomer also claimed to have seen such a planet passing in front of the sun. Sadly for Mr. Spock, however, Vulcan has never been seen since. The strange orbit of Mercury can be explained by the fact that the sun bends the space around the planet. Einstein's theory of relativity (see page 2) predicts this result. The search is still on for a group of supposed asteroids, named *vulcanoids* (vəl • kə • nōēdz), inside the orbit of Mercury.

THE RED PLANET

Mars has captured the imagination of artists, scholars, and astronomers for hundreds of years. Mars is 142 million miles (228 million km) from the sun. It takes Mars 687 Earth days to complete its orbit. It has a very thin atmosphere. In the Martian summer, dust storms cover the entire surface of the planet. The polar icecaps melt and re-form in the winter. The surface has a great variety of features, including dust dunes, craters, and the mighty Olympus Mons. Olympus Mons is an extinct volcano that measures 50 miles (80 km) across and 15.5 miles (25 km) high. There is some evidence that water once flowed on Mars. The image below of the surface of Mars was taken by the Viking probe. The probe landed on the planet in 1973. It took a series of stunning photographs.

THE ASTEROID BELT

A swarm of rocks with diameters from 0.6 to 620 miles (1 to 1,000 km) orbit the sun at distances ranging from 86 to 307 million miles (300 to 495 million km). These asteroids are very small by planetary standards and are irregular in shape. The Galileo probe produced this picture of the pitted, potato-shaped asteroid Gaspra from a distance of 1,000 miles (1,600 km). Even such small bodies as asteroids bear the scars of heavy meteorite crashes from the distant past.

SOME LIKE IT HOT

Mercury is the closest planet to the sun. Mercury orbits the sun once every 88 days at a distance of nearly 37 million miles (60 million km). Its day is 59 Earth days long. This was discovered using radar. In 1974, the *Mariner 10* spacecraft (spaceship) made this image of its surface. The photograph reveals a landscape more heavily cratered than the moon's. The surface temperature is over 400 degrees during the Mercurian day. It drops to almost 200 degrees below zero at night. Mercury has no atmosphere. The intense heat of the sun has boiled it away.

SCIENCE EXPLAINED: INTERPLANETARY TRAFFIC LAWS

The 17th-century German astronomer Johannes Kepler discovered three laws to explain how planets orbit:
1. A planet orbits the sun in an elliptical (i • lip • ti • kəl), oval shaped orbit.
2. Planets speed up as they get closer to the sun, and slow down as they get farther away.
3. The distance of a planet from the sun can be figured out. We need to know the length of its year, and the length of year and distance from the sun of one other planet (usually the Earth).

Great Dark Spot

NEPTUNE

Neptune is the farthest major planet from the sun. It takes 165 Earth years to complete an orbit around the sun. Neptune was discovered in 1846 after its position had been predicted by John Couch Adams in England and Urbain de Leverrier in France. Adams and de Leverrier figured out Neptune's position by the way it pulled on the neighboring planet, Uranus. Neptune is similar in structure to Uranus and has a prominent storm zone called the Great Dark Spot.

URANUS

In the right conditions, Uranus is just visible to the naked eye. It was discovered in 1781 by Sir William Herschel. It orbits the sun once every 84 Earth years. It spins almost on its side. Its seasons are strange: summer and winter each last 20 years. The planet's rocky core is surrounded by a thick shell of ice and the atmosphere is similar to that of Jupiter.

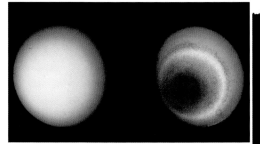

SCIENCE EXPLAINED: MASSES & DENSITIES

Astronomers are very interested in discovering the density of a planet. A simple equation allows them to work it out: the amount of mass divided by the space (volume) the planet occupies. Astronomers know the masses and the sizes of the planets from telescopic observations and information sent back by space probes. From this information, they can work out the densities. The Earth is about five times denser than water, which is typical of the terrestrial planets. Jupiter, Uranus, and Neptune are slightly denser than water. Saturn is actually less dense than water.

TOMBAUGH'S FIND

Pluto is farther from the sun than Uranus. It was discovered in 1930 by Clyde Tombaugh (*left*). Its position had been predicted earlier by Percival Lowell. Tombaugh's planet was smaller and closer to the sun than Lowell had predicted. Pluto is an icy world that is smaller than our moon, and yet it has its own satellite. This satellite, Charon, was discovered by James Walter Christy in 1978. Scientists used to think Pluto was a planet, but now it is considered a "minor planet."

GIANTS OF GAS & ICE

Beyond Mars and the asteroid belt lie four giant worlds that dwarf the Earth and its close neighbors. These are the mighty planets Jupiter, Saturn, Uranus, and Neptune. These giants all have rings and many moons. With the exception of Uranus, they all give out more heat than they receive from the sun. Out beyond the orbit of Neptune is the small double-world of Pluto-Charon.

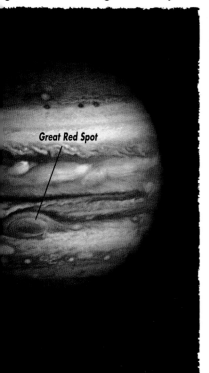

Great Red Spot

THE MOONS OF THE GIANTS

All four giant planets have large families of moons, some bigger than Mercury. Information from space probes has shown a surprising range among these minor worlds. Jupiter's moon Io (*above*) is the most volcanically active world in the solar system. The lava spouting from Io's volcanoes lands on the surface as solid lumps at the same speed as bullets from a machine gun. After Venus, Io is the most dangerous, changing world in the solar system.

THE KING OF PLANETS

Jupiter takes 12 Earth years to complete its orbit. It is the largest of the planets and it is big enough to swallow a thousand Earths. In fact, this giant has over twice the mass of all the other planets put together. Its rocky core is surrounded by a shell of liquid hydrogen. There is no solid surface. The thick, deep atmosphere contains mainly hydrogen and helium. The famous Great Red Spot is actually a violent storm that has been raging for centuries. The image on the left shows the planet with three of its moons—Io, Europa, and Ganymede.

THE RINGED PLANET

Saturn is the second largest of the planets. It takes just over 29 Earth years to complete an orbit. Because it is less dense than water, it would float if enough water could be found to run a bath for this giant! The most striking feature of Saturn is its beautiful ring system. The rings are actually made of millions of small chunks of rock and ice. *Voyager* probes revealed that there are actually hundreds of separate ringlets. They are divided into six groups, as shown in the false-color image on the right.

F RING—
the outermost ring

A RING—*the outermost ring visible from Earth*

CASSINI DIVISION—
although it appears to be a gap, this region contains over 100 faint rings

B RING—*the brightest and densest of the rings*

C RING—*this blue ring is the faintest visible from Earth*

D RING—*this faint ring almost touches Saturn*

SOLAR SYSTEM SMALL FRY

After the solar system was created about 4,500 million years ago, a lot of debris was left behind. The heavily cratered faces of the inner four planets and the moons of the giants came from a violent period of "mopping up." At this time, leftover space objects fell into the gravitational clutches of the planets and their moons. But the space between the planets and beyond is still full of a wide variety of small objects. These objects include comets, asteroids, and dust. They provide important clues to unraveling the mystery of the origin of the Earth and other planets.

SPACE ALERT

It is now widely accepted that the disappearance of the dinosaurs 60 million years ago was caused by a large meteorite crashing into the Earth. Films such as *Deep Impact* (*above*) reflect the disaster that might happen if our planet were ever to be struck again. The possible threat from comets and meteorites is taken seriously by astronomers and governments alike. The sky is now being monitored for so-called near-Earth objects to provide warnings of possible future threats to Earth.

The sun

Neptune's orbit

ASTEROIDS & METEORITES

Asteroids are rocks left over from when the planets were formed. They are found mainly between the orbits of Mars and Jupiter. *Meteorites* are chunks of stone that have broken off from asteroids and fall from space to Earth. Sometimes they are big enough to leave large craters, like the Barringer Crater in Arizona (*left*). The Barringer Crater measures over 0.6 miles (1 km) across. It was created 50,000 years ago by the *impact* (force) of a 165-foot-wide meteorite striking the Earth. The explosion was as large as 20 megatons of TNT blowing up.

COSMIC CRASHES

Cosmic disasters are not limited to the Earth. In July 1994, Comet Shoemaker-Levy 9 split into many fragments that hit Jupiter. The dark stains on these four images of Jupiter are the impact sites (where an object crashed). An event such as this on Earth would cause a huge amount of damage.

COMETS

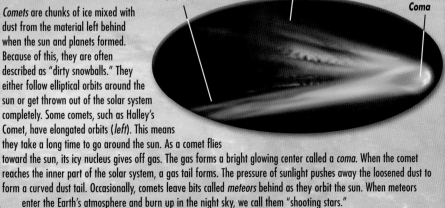

Gas tail

Dust tail

Coma

Pluto's orbit

Comets are chunks of ice mixed with dust from the material left behind when the sun and planets formed. Because of this, they are often described as "dirty snowballs." They either follow elliptical orbits around the sun or get thrown out of the solar system completely. Some comets, such as Halley's Comet, have elongated orbits (*left*). This means they take a long time to go around the sun. As a comet flies toward the sun, its icy nucleus gives off gas. The gas forms a bright glowing center called a *coma*. When the comet reaches the inner part of the solar system, a gas tail forms. The pressure of sunlight pushes away the loosened dust to form a curved dust tail. Occasionally, comets leave bits called *meteors* behind as they orbit the sun. When meteors enter the Earth's atmosphere and burn up in the night sky, we call them "shooting stars."

HYDROGEN INTO HELIUM

The huge amount of energy needed by the sun is produced by a complex process. In this process, hydrogen is changed into helium (see also page 8). This can be explained by Einstein's theory that a small mass loss creates large amounts of energy. In the case of the sun, this process gives an incredible amount of energy. It gives off so much energy that the sun is able to burn at a temperature of 15 million degrees at its core.

PROTON

NEUTRON

1. Two hydrogen protons join together to form a hydrogen proton-neutron pair called deuterium (dū • *tēr* • ē • əm).

HELIUM³

2. This pair is then joined by another hydrogen proton to make the nucleus of a helium³ atom.

3. Next, two helium³ nuclei (nū • klē • ī) join together to produce one stable helium atom (like the helium used to heat hot-air balloons).

STABLE HELIUM

PROTON

4. Because the mass of the four protons in the stable helium atom is too high, two protons are given off, creating energy. The spare protons then take part in future reactions.

THE SUN

The sun is a star that gives heat and light to the solar system. It is a huge fiery gas ball over 300,000 times the size of the Earth. By changing hydrogen to helium, it makes large amounts of energy. This hydrogen burning is the same reaction that occurs in hydrogen bombs. Without this energy, there would be no life on Earth. The sun burns 400 tons of hydrogen in a second, but thankfully there is enough left to last another 5,000 million years!

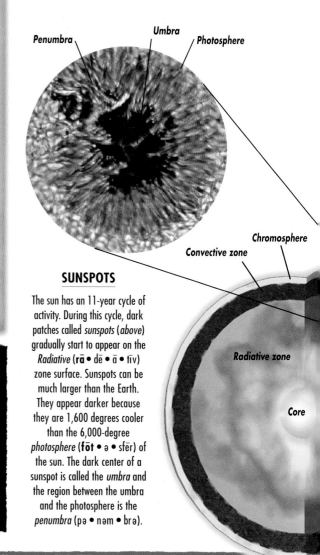

Penumbra   Umbra   Photosphere

Chromosphere

Convective zone

Radiative zone

Core

SUNSPOTS

The sun has an 11-year cycle of activity. During this cycle, dark patches called *sunspots* (*above*) gradually start to appear on the *Radiative* (rā • dē • ā • tiv) zone surface. Sunspots can be much larger than the Earth. They appear darker because they are 1,600 degrees cooler than the 6,000-degree *photosphere* (**fōt** • ə • sfēr) of the sun. The dark center of a sunspot is called the *umbra* and the region between the umbra and the photosphere is the *penumbra* (pə • nəm • brə).

ANGRY ERUPTIONS

Prominences (**prô** • mə • nən • səz) are giant clouds that arch over the sun and then fall back to its surface. They are far less energetic than flares and look dark when seen against the photosphere. This picture (*right*) shows a very active sun with a very large prominence. The Earth would be a mere speck in comparison to this mighty eruption.

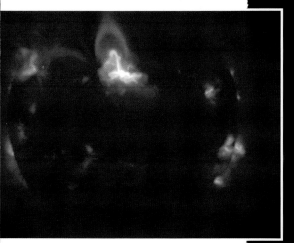

FLARES & SPACE WEATHER

A flare is a very energetic explosion that begins in the *chromosphere* (**krō** • mə • sfēr) of the sun. A flare gets bigger when it reaches the *corona* (kə • **rō** • nə). Flares give off very high energy X-rays and charged particles that reach Earth and occasionally cause problems with communications. This amazing flare (*above*) is seen ripping its way through the corona. Flares are so dangerous that the sun's activity is monitored daily by the Space Environment Center.

STRUCTURE OF THE SUN

Sunlight has a hard time reaching us. After it is forged in the core of the sun, it gets bounced about for a million years in what is called the *radiative zone*. Then it has to go through the bubbling convective zone before finally reaching the *photosphere*. The photosphere is the part of the sun's surface that we see. Above the photosphere, there is the thick lower atmosphere called the *chromosphere*. Above that, and stretching beyond the Earth, is the thin *corona*. We see the visible part of the corona during an eclipse.

Photosphere

THE MILKY WAY & OTHER GALAXIES

THE MILKY WAY

The Milky Way has interested humans for thousands of years, but it was Galileo (*above*) who first observed it through a telescope. He found that it was made of millions of stars. Parts of the Milky Way can easily be seen in the night sky (see pages 6–7). Through a pair of binoculars you can see that it is actually made up of clusters of faint stars. We can only see a bit of the Milky Way, however, because most of our galaxy is blotted out by dust. Astronomers use radio waves to "see" the whole picture.

It was only in the 20th century that people discovered that we live in a galaxy that is merely one among countless others. *Galaxies* are vast star systems and are the largest individual bodies in the universe. There are many different types of galaxy, from dwarf types to giant galaxies. Some show violent activity at their centers, where there are massive black holes (see page 24).

SCIENCE EXPLAINED:
MAPPING OUR GALAXY WITH RADIO WAVES

Radio waves are so long that they can pass through the clouds of dust that hide most of our galaxy from view. Free hydrogen atoms in space send radio waves at a wavelength of 8 inches (21 cm). If the atom giving off the radio waves is moving away from us, this will cause the wavelength to appear slightly longer. If the source is coming toward us, the wavelength will be shorter. This lets radio astronomers map galaxies. The method has been used to reveal the long spiral arms of the Milky Way stretching outwards to the edge of the disc.

QUASARS

These astronauts are holding a model of the Chandra X-Ray Observatory. The observatory is expected to allow researchers to get much better x-ray images of *quasars* (kwā • zärz). Quasars are a mystery. They are so far away from us that they look like very faint stars. In reality, they are blazing beacons as bright as an entire galaxy. Quasars are located in the most distant reaches of the universe.

Elliptical

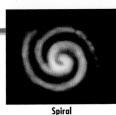

Spiral

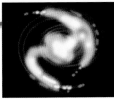

Barred Spiral

Irregular

THE GALAXY ZOO

Edwin Hubble classified galaxies into elliptical, spiral, barred, and irregular types. Almost three-quarters of the galaxies in the universe are elliptical. These are shaped like eggs. *Spiral galaxies* have a familiar shape, with the arms emerging from the central bulge. The Milky Way is a spiral galaxy. *Barred galaxies* are similar in shape but have a central bridge of stars linking the inner ends of the spiral arms. Finally, *irregular galaxies* are galaxies that do not fit into any of these shapes.

THE MILKY WAY: AN ARTIST'S IMPRESSION

We cannot see very deeply into the Milky Way without the use of infrared and radio-wave technology. This is because of the large amount of dust from inside the disc region. This illustration shows what our galaxy probably looks like when seen from above. The central bulge contains stars but almost no gas or dust. The disc region contains spiral arms that contain gas, dust, and young stars. Our solar system is located somewhere in the Orion arm.

Bulge

Disc region

Orion arm

STELLAR POPULATIONS

During World War II, the German astronomer Walter Baade discovered that stars are distributed in galaxies according to age. In spiral galaxies such as ours, young stars (together with the giant clouds from which they were born) appear in the disc region. The bulge is full of old stars. In elliptical galaxies all the stars are old. Baade laid the foundations for all future work on the life histories of stars and galaxies with his findings. In the galaxy NGC 2997 (*right*), we see the young (blue) stars of the disc region and the old (yellow) stars of the bulge.

Bulge   *Disc region*

DEADLY HOLES

Sometimes a supernova explosion leaves behind a piece that is too massive even for a neutron star. When this happens, the star disappears and becomes a *black hole*. The nucleus gets crushed into such a tiny volume that the extreme gravitational pull of the core closes up the space around it. This prevents even light from escaping.

Black holes cannot be seen, but their presence can be detected. They swallow surrounding matter. The matter spirals into the black hole and forms a disc that gets so hot that it gives off X-rays. These can be detected by space probes. As you approach a black hole you start to feel its gravitational pull get stronger. The closer you get, the more speed you will need to escape its tight clutches. If you were silly enough to enter the barrier of blackness known as the event horizon, you would never get out again.

Outer region

Middle region

Inner region

Electrons

Atomic nuclei

NEUTRON STARS

Neutron stars are born when gravity forces a star to collapse so much that its electrons are forced together inside the atomic nuclei (*see above*). The neutron star can be as small as 19 miles (30 km) across. They have strong magnetic fields and spin very quickly. Some spin more than a hundred times per second. Neutron stars are also magnetic. These two things cause them to give off their light in the form of two beams on opposite sides of the star (*right*). Neutron stars whose beams we can see are called *pulsars* (pəl • särz).

COSMIC PUZZLERS

When stars like the sun die, they end their days as *white dwarfs*. Stars that start out ten times bigger than the sun, however, meet a very different fate. The pieces left after such explosions are far denser than white dwarfs. They can become either small superdense objects called neutron stars or black holes. Black holes suck matter out of the universe, like huge whirlpools. Even stranger are *wormholes*. They are thought to link parts of the universe by time tunnels that might make time travel possible.

EXPLOSION!

Supergiant stars rush through their fuel supply and die in a massive explosion that outshines a billion suns. Two things happen during this type of supernova explosion. First, the outer shell of gas is blasted away, as shown in this picture of the Crab Nebula. There is also an inward implosion, which compresses the star's core to even higher densities than those of white dwarfs. At this point the core will become either a neutron star or a black hole.

TIME TRAVELER

Many science fiction films explore the possibility of time travel. In *The Terminator*, a deadly robot is sent back in time. Although this is science fantasy, some astronomers believe that time travel might be possible. There are things in space called wormholes. These are supposed to connect distant parts of the universe by a kind of tunnel in space-time. Just like in a black hole, time slows to a standstill, and the known laws of the universe stop working. If a wormhole could be kept open long enough, it might be possible to travel through unharmed.

WHERE DID IT ALL BEGIN?

Some astronomers, such as Sir Fred Hoyle (*far right*), believe that life started before Earth was formed. They argue that the chances of DNA-type molecules evolving from simple carbon molecules are far too slim. They believe that this could only have happened long before the Earth was created. The Big Bang Theory claims that the universe is 15,000 million years old (see pages 28–29). If this theory is correct, astronomers believe that there would have been enough time for DNA to evolve in space. Life molecules would then have been delivered to the Earth by close-approaching comets. This idea is called the *Panspermia Theory* (pan • spər • **mē** • ə **thē** • rē).

LIFE NOT AS WE KNOW IT

Science fiction writers have invented all sorts of strange beings to populate the universe. E.T. (*right*), the *extraterrestrial* (**ek** • strə • tə • **res** • trē • əl) from the Steven Spielberg blockbuster, is one. All known forms of life are based on the carbon atom, so astronomers look for traces of carbon-based molecules elsewhere in the galaxy. They have been found in comets, meteorites, and the clouds from which stars form. The existence of life elsewhere is still debated.

LOOKING FOR E.T.

Is there other intelligent life in the universe? Have we been visited by extraterrestrials? Some have claimed that spacemen built the Egyptian pyramids. Possible flying saucer sightings are regularly reported. An astronomer's answer to all this is to point out that, as far as we know, nothing can travel faster than light. The distances between stars are simply too large for such travel to be possible.

AN INTELLIGENT UNIVERSE

An idea that has had a lot of attention from astronomers over recent years is that the universe is built in a way that demands the existence of human life. This is called the *Anthropic Principle* (an • **thrä** • pik   **prin** • si • pəl). Going even further, the British astronomer Sir Fred Hoyle (*above*) has suggested that human intelligence is part of a chain of intelligences. According to Hoyle, the universe itself is at the top of the chain.

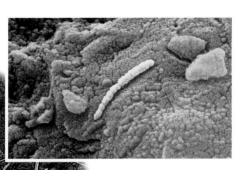

IS ANYBODY THERE?

The discovery of a simple, single-celled organism inside a meteorite from Mars (*above*) was greeted with wild enthusiasm by astronomers. Most of us are really interested in knowing whether there are other intelligent beings in space. A project called *SETI* (Search for Extraterrestrial Intelligence) has been set up. This searches the sky with the largest radio telescope in the world at Arecibo in Puerto Rico (*left*). The amount of data gathered is huge. The SETI program has invited all owners of computers to download SETI software to help look for signals from extraterrestrials.

SCIENCE EXPLAINED: TRAVELING TO THE STARS

To give an idea of how difficult travel between the stars is, imagine that we could make our spaceships travel at 660 miles (1,100 km) per second. This is a hundred times faster than the speed needed to escape the Earth's pull. Even traveling that fast, it would still take 1,000 years to reach the nearest star, just a few light years away! Our galaxy is 100,000 light years wide. Our spaceship would take 25 million years to cross it. So unless extraterrestrials have far more advanced technology than we do, they are not likely to reach us in the near future.

HOW WILL IT ALL END?

What will be the fate of the universe? Everything depends on how dense the universe is. There are three possibilities. If the density is higher than a certain value (the critical density), then the universe will eventually stop expanding and collapse in on itself. This is called the Big Crunch *Scenario* (sə • nā̄ • r • ē • ō). If the density is less than critical, then the universe will just go on expanding. The temperature of everything in the universe will drop. Everything will become freezing cold. This scenario is called the Heat Death Scenario. Finally, if the density is just borderline, the universe will expand less and less but will not collapse. This is called the Flat Universe Scenario. Boomerang (*left*), a balloon experiment sent high into the atmosphere above the Antarctic, measured the "bumpiness" in the cosmic background. This measurement shows that the universe is actually flat. In other words, neither the Big Crunch nor the Heat Death scenario will happen.

SCIENCE EXPLAINED: HUBBLE'S LAW

Edwin Hubble was the first to suggest that the galaxies are moving away from us. This idea was later developed into the theory of the expanding universe. Hubble also discovered that the speed at which a galaxy moves away from us depends on its distance. The farther away from us a galaxy is, the faster it moves. This important law can be used to find the distance of a galaxy by using its speed as it travels away.

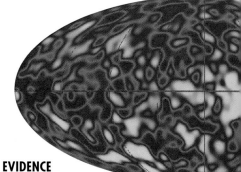

OTHER EVIDENCE

Apart from the expansion of the universe, there are other important pieces of evidence in favor of the Big Bang theory. After any explosion, a fireball expands and cools. In the case of the Big Bang, the original fireball occurred about 15 billion years ago. It should by now have a temperature of 270 degrees below zero. The image of the universe taken by the COBE satellite (*above right*) confirmed this temperature.

EXPANSION OF THE UNIVERSE

The galaxies all appear to be moving away from us at very high speeds. This is not because we are in any special position in the universe. Exactly the same thing would be observed from any other galaxy. In fact, it is not the galaxies that are moving, but the space between them that is expanding. Imagine sticking stars on a balloon and then blowing the balloon up. The stars would seem to move apart as the balloon inflates. The expansion of the universe is a process that has been occurring over billions of years.

THE BIG BANG & THE FATE OF THE UNIVERSE

One of the key problems that cosmologists are always trying to solve is how the universe was created. They believe that the universe came into being about 15 billion years ago in a huge explosion called the *Big Bang*. From being squashed together in a tight ball, matter suddenly expanded outward. Eventually, the stars and planets were created. Astronomers are also trying to work out how the universe will end, and have come up with a number of different ideas.

THE BEGINNING OF EVERYTHING

If the universe is expanding, could this mean that the galaxies started out from a dense clump of matter at some time in the past? Imagine filming the explosion of a bomb in the air. After the explosion, we see fragments of the bomb rushing away from one another. If we rewind the film, we will come to the original unexploded bomb. Most astronomers now believe that the expansion of the universe started from the explosion of a fireball some 15 billion years ago. This explosion is known as the Big Bang.

CREATING CONDITIONS FOR LIFE

Today, conditions on Earth are perfect for life, allowing a huge variety of creatures to thrive. However, these conditions have taken billions of years to evolve. Astronomers believe the universe has gone through several stages since the Big Bang. At first, the fireball was 10 billion degrees. After 30,000 years the temperature dropped to 10,000 degrees, still far too hot for life. During this period, called the "radiation era," matter and radiation formed a very thick soup. After the radiation era came the "matter era." At this time, matter became separated from the radiation. The universe became transparent and its temperature dropped to the present chilly 270 degrees below zero.

ASTRONOMY TODAY & IN THE FUTURE

Civilians (non-astronauts) have been going into space for some years now. Dennis Tito's trip in 2001 was very different. Tito paid his own fare—some 20 million dollars! There is now an International Space Station in Earth orbit. Its living quarters are (so far) for working astronauts, and were not meant to be a hotel for tourists. Now other *millionaires* (mil • yə • **nār**z) are lining up for a once-in-a-lifetime space trip. It is likely that before the century is over, ordinary people will be able to fly to the moon, Mars, and maybe beyond.

f astronomy today looks exciting, astronomy in the future will be truly mouthwatering! Major advances are being made on a regular basis. New giant telescopes are being built to help astronomers look farther into space. New sites for telescopes are being planned in the Antarctic to take advantage of the excellent conditions there. The future also looks likely to bring an observatory on the moon and possibly even Mars. Yet this is only the beginning for the astronomy of tomorrow. There is even talk of sending a space submarine to Jupiter's moon Europa to probe for life in its frozen oceans.

A SUBMARINE TO EUROPA?

Europa is bathed in dangerous radiation from Jupiter. Even though its environment is harsh, astronomers are excited to go there. They think that there are oceans beneath its frozen surface. Some kind of robotic submarine probe could be sent from Earth to explore Europa's oceans for possible life. These oceans would be in permanent darkness because of the thickness of the ice above them. However, the bottoms of the Earth's oceans are always dark, and yet there is life there. Seven-foot-long worms have been found near volcanic vents on the ocean beds.

GREAT ARRAY

The ability of a telescope to display fine detail is decided by the width of its primary mirror. If two telescopes are used together they only collect as much light as the total size of the two mirrors will allow. However, their ability to display fine detail is determined by the distance between them. Large *arrays*, or sets, of optical and radio telescopes have already been built. There are plans to build even better ones in the future. Besides the high mountain sites in La Palma and Hawaii, astronomers have also begun to build these telescopes in the Antarctic. With its very dry air, providing excellent conditions for infrared work, Antarctica looks set to become more important in the future of astronomy.

A LUNAR OBSERVATORY?

With a permanent manned base on the moon, astronomers will almost certainly put large telescopes there. The main benefit to astronomers from permanent space observatories is that they will always be able to use all parts of the spectrum. This includes wavelengths in the infrared, ultraviolet, x-ray, and gamma ray regions (see pages 4–5). For the near future, there are several large space projects being planned.

GLOSSARY

Asteroids—Lumps of rock left over when the planets in the solar system were formed. They are mostly found in a zone called the asteroid belt between Mars and Jupiter.

Atom—The smallest chemical unit of matter, made up of a nucleus surrounded by orbiting electrons.

Black hole—Superdense object with such a high concentration of matter and gravity that not even light can escape.

Comet—A chunk of ice and dust that orbits the sun.

Constellation—A grouping of stars in the sky, named after characters in Greek and Roman mythology.

Density—The amount of mass divided by the amount of space an object occupies.

Dwarf—The name given to a newly formed star when it begins to convert its hydrogen into helium.

Einstein's theory of relativity—Theory of gravity devised by Albert Einstein (1879–1955) that applies to massive objects with intense gravitational fields.

Electron—A negatively charged particle that orbits a nucleus.

Galaxy—A gigantic gathering of stars, the biggest single unit in the universe.

Galaxy cluster—A collection of galaxies. A really large grouping is called a supercluster.

Giant—A swollen star that has left the main sequence.

Globular cluster—A grouping of up to 100,000 old stars tightly bound together by gravity.

Luminosity—The amount of radiation given off at the surface of a star or planet.

Meteor—Debris left behind by comets, visible as a bright vapor trail when it enters the Earth's atmosphere.

Meteorite—A chunk of rock that has broken off from asteroids and fallen to Earth.

Molecule—A clump of two or more atoms.

Neutron—A neutral particle forming part of the atomic nucleus.

Neutron star—An incredibly dense star left over from the explosion of a supernova.

Newton's theory of gravity—Theory devised by Sir Isaac Newton (1642–1727) stating that all objects are attracted to each other. The attraction is stronger for more massive objects. However, this attraction diminishes as objects get farther away from one another.

Open cluster—A large family of up to 10,000 young stars in the plane of the Milky Way.

Proton—A positively charged particle forming part of the atomic nucleus.

Spectrum—The light from a star or galaxy split up into wavelengths of different colors.

Supergiant—A former hot, bright main sequence star that has swollen to many times its original size.

White dwarf—A dead star left behind in the center of a planetary nebula.

First published in Great Britain by ticktock Publishing Ltd. Printed in China.

ISBN-13: 978-1-59905-445-2   ISBN-10: 1-59905-445-0   eBook: 978-1-60291-771-2

15 14 13 12 11   1 2 3 4 5

t=top, b=bott c=center, l=left, r=right, OFC=outside front cover, IFC=inside front cover, IBC=inside back cover, OBC=outside back cover

Art Archive: 3br, 18tl, 22tl. Corbis Images: 16b, 19t, 27tr, 27t, 29b, 31t. Kobal Collection: 14c, 25b, 19b, 26b. NASA: 2tl, 3tr, 8cr, 9cl, 9b, 12cl, 12b, 13tr, 14tl, 15tl, 15cr, 15cl, 15c, 16tl, 16tr, 16–17c, 16br, 16tr, 16br, 17tr, 17br, 19cl, 20tl, 21tl, 23tr, 25tr. National Maritime Museum: 2bl. Popperfoto: 22b, 30tl. Science Photo Library: OBC, 21r, 26b, 26cl, 31b. Tony Stone: 12–13c.

Every effort has been made to trace the copyright holders and we apologize in advance for any unintentional omissions.
We would be pleased to insert the appropriate acknowledgement in any subsequent edition of this publication.

SADDLEBACK
EDUCATIONAL PUBLISHING